how to be a girl
THE COMMON SENSE GUIDE TO GIRLHOOD

ANITA NAIK

WAYLAND

First published in 2014 by Wayland
Copyright © Wayland 2014
Wayland
338 Euston Road
London NW1 3BH

Wayland Australia
Level 17/207
Kent Street
Sydney, NSW 2000

Editor: Debbie Foy
Designer: Simon Daley

Dewey ref: 305.2'352-dc23

ISBN 978 0 7502 8250 5
eBook ISBN 978 0 7502 8789 0

Printed in UK

10 9 8 7 6 5 4 3 2 1

Wayland is a division of Hachette Children's Books,
an Hachette UK company.
www.hachette.co.uk

how to be a girl

Dedicated to Bella and all her friends who
are just discovering what it means to be
a girl. Multiple thanks also to Debbie Foy
who came up with the idea for this book
and helped shape it so well. Thanks also
to Julie Sleaford and all the girls and
women who helped with this book.

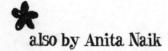

also by Anita Naik

Teen Life Confidential: Texts, Tweets, Trolls and Teens
Teen Life Confidential: Self-Esteem and Being YOU
Teen Life Confidential: Queen Bees, Drama Queens & Cliquey Teens
Teen Life Confidential: Sex, Snogs, Dates and Mates
Teen Life Confidential: Periods, Zits & Other Bits
Bras, Boys & Bad Hair Days
The Quick Expert's Guide to Safe Social Networking

contents

introduction

*'A girl should be two things:
who and what she wants.'

COCO CHANEL, FASHION DESIGNER

How to be a girl? It should be so easy shouldn't it? Just go out there and be yourself. Most of the time, that's how it is. It's fun and it's exciting and it's more than great to be a girl. Except that as you get older you start to notice that girls also have a lot of unfair pressure put on them. It can seem as if the world believes your worth is based on your looks rather than your abilities, and that your main job in life is to keep working at improving your imperfect body. Then there is the pressure to be 'girl perfect': to have lots of friends, have hundreds of followers on Instagram, get your quota of likes on Facebook and still do amazingly well at school! It can be exhausting and sometimes make you feel that being a girl is too much like hard work!

I've been an agony aunt for teenage girls for over 20 years and I can see from my inbox and postbag that never before has there been so much pressure on girls to look and behave in a certain way. The emails and letters I get tell a story of girls who feel under pressure. Girls who are tired of being told to worry about everything from their weight to their hair, to body parts you never even knew existed. Girls who feel under pressure to be pretty rather than smart. And girls who feel boxed into a corner at home and at school just because they happen to be a girl.

These girls are the reason *How To Be A Girl* came about. This book is about the very opposite of telling you what you have to be. Instead, it's a book about showing you how to be happier, more secure and confident. It's about finding solutions to things that get you down, feeling positive about your body and standing up to the inevitable pressures of being a girl.

Most of all, it's about finding the courage to discover your voice (you know, the big loud one that people might tell you to lower). For that reason it's scattered with tips, top role models to inspire you, advice to boost your self-esteem and ways to get informed. All so you can become 100% glad to be a girl!

anita x

how to be a girl

*The average girl worries about her looks every 15 minutes.

GRAZIA MAGAZINE

How to be a girl is such an obvious thing isn't it? So obvious there shouldn't even be a book about it. Just like being a boy: you should be able to get on with what you are doing and be the kind of person you want to be.

The problem is that the expectations and pressures on girls are increasing, so that although we live in a world where there are many opportunities for girls, some girls are being made to feel insecure about themselves. Instead of feeling excited by the opportunities open to them, many girls feel worried: worried about how they look, worried about how many friends they have and worried about how smart they need to be.

Being a teenager is a challenging as well as an exciting time, so it's normal to feel a bit uptight sometimes. What isn't acceptable is the criticism of those who try to do things their own way. So what's a girl to do? Well, the answer is to think about what being a girl means to you. Do others (friends, parents, people you don't know) dictate who you should be? Does the fact you have a spot on your nose utterly ruin

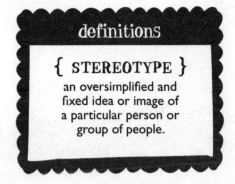

definitions

{ STEREOTYPE }

an oversimplified and fixed idea or image of a particular person or group of people.

your day? Or does a mean comment stop you from feeling good about who you are? If so, it's time to refuse to let others tell you what you can and can't be. It sounds impossible to do, but this book will show you how to handle these issues and more!

stereotypes 'r' us

Stereotypes are everywhere. Most are just silly, like the idea that people who wear glasses are clever, or girls with blonde hair are ditsy. Clearly, those cannot be true. Some stereotypes are more subtle, but they can be so strong that they can: (1) Stop you from doing the things you want to do (2) Make others judge you unfairly and (3) Push you in directions that you may not want to go in. For instance, you may avoid answering questions in class because you don't want to be stereotyped and made fun of for being a geek or a nerd, or perhaps you didn't join the football club because kids at school think football is only a boy's sport. Or maybe you're feeling the pressure to be interested in boys before you're ready, just because everyone seems to assume that all girls of a certain age can think about is boys and dating.

Unfortunately, girl stereotypes can start early in life. Ask your parents what you were like as a baby and they may well use words like 'sweet', 'gorgeous' and 'princess'. Think about the toys you played with when you were young. Was there an emphasis on pink, princesses and Barbie dolls? Toys might seem like harmless fun, but child development experts now believe that toys aimed at girls (unlike toys for boys, which are often about engineering, building and adventure) encourage girls to focus too much on their looks, clothes and appearance.

Even stereotypes that seem as if they are compliments can be a problem! When girls constantly hear comments like 'Girls are arty and creative', 'Girls are good at reading', or 'Girls are quieter, more helpful and better behaved than boys', it can stop them from daring to take risks, be adventurous and be loud and wild!

And of course, you can't escape from this world of stereotypes by turning on the TV. The images you see of girls on screen are too often painfully stereotypical – even on kids' TV where girl heroes are often shown as princesses, playing with cute animals or self-sacrificing mothers. It can sometimes feel as if there are stereotypes telling you what girls should be all over the media!

It also pays to acknowledge any preconceptions about girls that you may have. Do you believe certain things about what it means to be a girl? What are you bringing to the party in terms of rules and stereotypes for your friends and other girls?

Finally, if you want to break free of the stereotyped image of a girl who can't do anything without a boy then try not to fall for the endless 'girl as a victim' stories, songs and myths that tend to play a big part in fiction, film and television. This doesn't mean you have to give up what you like watching or reading – just look at broadening the scope of what you choose, so to give you a more balanced view of life. So, for example:

 Choose books with strong female characters, such as *Harriet The Spy* by Louise Fitzhugh, *Otherwise Known As Sheila The Great* by Judy Blume, *Secrets* by Jacqueline Wilson, *The Hunger Games Trilogy* by Suzanne Collins, *The Divergent Trilogy* by Veronica Roth, *Harry Potter* Series by JK Rowling, and *The Fault In Our Stars* by John Green. If you've read those, look up www.goodreads.com or Amazon to find lists of best teen girl books for more inspiration.

 Watch films that are about more than just 'girl meets boy'. There's a lot more to a girl's life than romance! Mix and match your viewing to give yourself a balanced perspective. Smart films are particularly good at making you think, for example: *Frozen* (2014), *Veronica Mars* (2014), *Divergent* (2014), *Brave* (2012), *10 Things I Hate About You* (1999), *Mean Girls* (2004), *Matilda* (2004) and *Mulan* (2004).

* Switch off so-called 'reality' shows. Okay, so these can be funny, but the women (and men) on these shows are usually chosen because they are exaggerated stereotypes and tend to play to the camera. Their words and encounters are often scripted anyway, so what you're watching isn't even real.

* Find some empowering role models. Role models can be anyone you admire in real life. If you're stuck for ideas, check out the 'Top Role Model' features in this book, such as Malala Yousafzai, who was shot in Pakistan over her fight for girls' educational rights, Angelina Jolie who campaigns for UNHCR and UNICEF, or girl blogger, writer and actress Tavi Gevinson. (For more on the power of role models see Chapter 4.)

* Choose to listen to music that empowers you, not music that belittles the idea of being female. Artists like Beyonce, Adele, Haim, Lorde, Amanda Mair all have something interesting to say. However, it doesn't have to be a female singer or group that empowers you. The lyrics and music of any band male or female can work for you as long as it's music that makes you feel strong not weak.

be the boss of you!

STAND UP TO STEREOTYPES

Here are some ideas for standing up to girl stereotypes.

1 Never just accept what others say as a girl truth – lots of people try to back up their stereotypes with facts and beliefs that are not true. So if someone tells you that being a girl means not being good at science, don't believe it. It's easy to disprove what they say with a quick Google search into all the women who are good at science and tech.

2 Don't let others try to define you or tell you what it means to be a girl. Only you get to decide what being a girl means to you. So what if people often say that all girls love shopping? The reality is some do, some don't.

3 Consider all the many ways to make a stand. You don't have to be confrontational or argumentative. You can simply make your own decisions in your head and stick to them. Or slowly try to make small changes around you and build up to the big ones.

4 You can challenge the stereotypes in quiet ways too. Sometimes this just means simply ignoring what's being said. For instance, if someone insists that all boys are faster or smarter than girls, let it go. You know the truth so why bother to argue?

5 Talk about it. Ask people outright why they think being a geek is a bad thing or being a girl is worse than being a boy. Sometimes just questioning what someone is saying and talking about it, makes others see that they are wrong.

are you falling for stereotypes?

Sometimes it can be hard to work out whether you're being placed under pressure or not. Try our quick quiz to see if you're falling for stereotypes.

1 A pop star that you admire has put on weight. Do you…

a Go off her as she's not as pretty as she once was
b Stand up for her as everyone on social media is slating her
c Get annoyed that people are making fun of her but say nothing?

2 People like you because…

a You're nice and you make an effort to get along with everyone
b You're attractive and popular
c You have no idea?

3 You believe girls should dress...

a The way they want

b The way all their friends do

c As fashionably as they can.

4 A boy you like says he hates it when girls wear trainers. Do you...

a Carry on wearing trainers. That's your style!

b Decide never to wear them again. They obviously don't look good.

c Only wear trainers when he's not around?

5 The best films are the ones that have...

a Great female characters who carry the movie

b A girl who gets the boy she wants

c Lots of action and hunky men

scores

1 A 0 B 10 C 5
2 A 10 B 5 C 0
3 A 10 B 5 C 0
4 A 10 B 0 C 5
5 A 10 B 0 C 5

results

0 – 15 *You tend to follow stereotypes of what it means to be a girl. It makes you feel safe and popular and works for you. That's fair enough, but are you really being true to yourself? Sometimes, wearing what you want or saying what you want, or liking someone who's not popular can be more empowering and make you feel stronger than you think.*

20 – 35 *You tend to conform to stereotypes but you're starting to break free of them. Remember, to do this you don't have to be confrontational. Make a stand in your own way. You could start with small things, like admitting you don't like the same film as your mates or maybe dressing a bit differently from your family and friends. In time these small changes will help your confidence grow and you'll be able to make bigger and bigger stands for what you believe in.*

40 – 50 *You definitely do not let stereotypes fence you in! You are your own person on the inside and outside. You choose to act and dress how you want and follow who you want, no matter what others say. Remember, standing up for yourself doesn't mean you have to feel like an outsider. Look around and find people who think and feel the same way as you – they are out there.*

family views of girlhood

Our family's beliefs and expectations (especially their cultural ones) have a strong effect on our own ideas about what it means to be a girl. This is often a good thing as it gives us a fast track to knowing what it means to be a good, smart person. However, even if you're lucky enough to have the most understanding parents in the world, all parents have their own ideas of what's good for girls and what isn't. Sometimes these ideas come from how and where they grew up and by the era in which they were born.

If you ask your mum and granny what was expected of them when they were growing up, you might be surprised by some of the things they say. Luckily, some old-fashioned ideas, like girls not having careers, not being paid the same as men, not going to university or not staying single, are not as common now as they were when your gran was growing up!

However, other ideas about what girls should be and how they should behave are still around. For instance, some parents have very different attitudes about how girls and boys should behave, and they may have been passing these on to you since you were little. You may have grown up getting the message that as a girl you're supposed to be 'quiet and helpful'. Or that being a daredevil is a dangerous business for girls, while boys are allowed or even expected to take more risks. Most of the time, parents are simply concerned and want to protect you and keep you safe from the potential dangers they see in the outside world. The trouble is that this can make them (and you!) think of girls as helpless and vulnerable. This, in turn, can have a huge impact on how you view the world and the type of girl you think you should be.

One of the most important ways that you learn about what it means to be a girl is from the examples your parents set you, in the ways they behave and their beliefs about what being a girl or woman means in this world. This doesn't mean that all of their ideas about womanhood are old-fashioned or wrong, but that you need to be aware of the messages they may be (unintentionally) sending in your direction about school expectations, your intelligence, body image and the way that you should behave.

For instance, if you have a brother consider how your mum and dad behave around you both. Do they treat you the same way or expect different things from you? How do your parents talk about being clever and smart? Does your dad infer that he's cleverer or can park better than your mum (even jokingly), or does your mum give you messages that she thinks girls and boys are different when it comes to doing certain physical or mental tasks?

Who works in your family? Do both your parents have jobs they consider important? Are they positive about girls and careers and what you can do in life? Or do you get a completely different message about the kinds of jobs girls can do compared to boys?

When it comes to challenging how to be a girl at home this can be tricky, particularly when your parents have a strong belief that comes from their own background and upbringing. The key here is not to be argumentative, but to realise that there are many ways to stand up for what you believe in. Simply deciding you're going to be different or live a different life when you're older is enough for many girls. If, however, you feel you need to be bolder, think about starting with small changes that are less challenging to your parents and build to the big ones over time. For instance, if your parents are very strict about you going out after school, maybe you could start off by joining an after-school club once a week.

Then maybe later they might let you go to the cinema with friends as well. Or you could start to talk about what you would like to be when you are older. This is less challenging (and more important) than arguing with them now about the type of clothes you want to wear or whether you are allowed to wear make-up!

girls' views on girlhood

How do you see the other girls in your life? As equals and as good as the boys you know, or as girlie girls, tomboys, swots, or flirts? We're all guilty of categorizing each other and that includes girls.

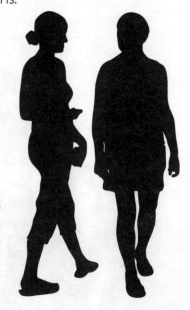

But girls need to think more about the way they see each other, not least because studies have found that your friendships will play as big a role in how you feel about your body, your life and what it means to be a girl as TV and social media.

You may not think your friends influence you in any way, but think about how you dress, how you act, what you believe about yourself, and how you talk about other girls and it's likely that you and your friends are all on the same page.

Whether you like it or not, it's your friends and all the other girls in your life (from the 'queen bees' right through to the outsiders) who give you strong rules about what it means to be a girl. This also means that these are the girls who will judge you if you fail to live up to their idea of being a girl.

Sometimes, other people's expectations can inspire us to be better, but even if girls you know don't always get it right, there's no need to abandon your friends! Just try to be more tuned in to what they are saying and doing around you. Try not to take on board the beliefs that don't sit right with you, especially those that judge other girls for their behaviour and looks. And think about how you talk about other girls and women – and not just the ones you know.

let's big up girls!

Are you hypercritical of other girls' bodies and so-called flaws? Do you judge them on how they look? Do you call them names when they annoy you? Are you quick to condemn them if they break a rule around boys and dating? Do you treat them more harshly than boys? If so, it's probably time to rethink your own behaviour.

Being a girl is about many things but it's also about

supporting other girls and being a girl who likes girls. It's not about turning against each other to score points or approval from others and it's not a competition in which every other girl is the enemy. Why? Well, because the first step towards feeling strong is about standing up for the girls who are different from you and not playing the popularity or exclusion game.

Life is a lot better when we're not all judging each other for the worst. So, whether a girl likes to wear short skirts or flirt with boys, or excel at maths and science or play sports, remember she's a girl just like you and you should respect her for her choices, as you'd want her to respect you for yours!

You can make a difference. Here's how!

* Avoid being a part of the gossip mill even for a laugh (online and offline).

* Compliment other girls – it makes both of you feel good.

* Find some inspiring role models amongst the friends you have and the women you know.

* If someone says girls can't do something, show them that you can!

* Read up on inspiring famous women and tell your friends about them. It's one of the best ways to feel great about being a girl.

media views about being a girl

How do you feel women are represented on TV and on film? Is there a fair balance of men and women of all ages and looks? If you look at presenters, most female TV presenters tend to pretty, slim and young compared to male TV presenters who tend to fill the spectrum from young and good looking to old and argumentative.

> "'Fat' is usually the first insult a girl throws at another girl when she wants to hurt her. I mean is 'fat' really the worst thing a human being can be? Is 'fat' worse than 'vindictive', 'jealous', 'shallow', 'vain', 'boring' or 'cruel'? Not to me."
>
> J.K. ROWLING, AUTHOR

As for girl characters on TV shows, they tend to be one of two extremes: either quiet and passive or wild and out of control. Think of female characters on soap operas or comedies and think of the famous women who are in the media all the time and you'll see that they pretty much fit the stereotypes above.

What's all this got to do with being a girl? Well, quite a lot really. What we see tends to affect what we believe and how we feel we should act in life. If time and again we see that the quiet, nice girl always gets the guy while the mouthy girl always gets into trouble, the message is clear. What's more, when successful women are applauded for their looks (Jessica Ennis) and even their upper arms (Michelle Obama) instead of for their work and skills, it can give girls the idea that looking good is the only way to get anywhere in this world.

What's the solution? Well it doesn't mean switching off the shows you love, but making sure that you are being inspired by a variety of real women as well as the characters you see on TV.

Think of women you know, women in your family, women in politics, teachers you rate and even your friends. At the same time, try to widen your viewing habits so you see women represented in many different ways on TV, such as in the news, in documentaries, in comedies and everything else.

the truth about intelligence

Thankfully you don't need to be a rocket scientist to know that intelligence has nothing to do with being a boy or girl. Yet some people still seem to believe that males and females think differently and that one sex is smarter than the other in certain tasks or topics. But here's the truth about intelligence. Behavioural differences

the big issue!

GIRLS + MATHS = SUCCESS

There is a mistaken but sadly common belief that girls aren't as good at maths as boys. Literacy, art and verbal skills are all seen as girls' specialities, whereas science and maths are for the boys. These outdated ideas are such a problem that educational experts are attempting to solve it by introducing national initiatives to encourage girls into science, technology, engineering and maths.

between men and women are not down to the brains inside our heads. They are down to things outside of us – things like stereotyping, social pressures and cultural beliefs. Female brains aren't inferior or different and boys aren't better at dealing with practical or mathematical things. None of our abilities should be defined by the fact we are male or female.

Chew on on this for a minute: in countries like China, India and South Korea, where there are fewer stereotyped beliefs about girls' academic and scientific abilities, girls perform better in maths and science than they do in the UK!

It seems unbelievable now, but in the not-too-distant past women weren't admitted into certain top-level universities and schools in the UK. In fact, in some countries and some families the myth that men are smarter than women is still thought of as a truth and in some places in the world girls aren't even allowed to go to school. (Read about teenager Malala who is fighting for education rights in Pakistan on page 102.)

And don't think that these out-dated ideas aren't affecting you. If you feel you always need to ask a guy what he thinks rather than trust your own judgment or feel that somehow your dad knows more than your mum, you're falling for the old boys-are-smarter-than-girls scenario.

How can you kick yourself out of this way of thinking? One way is to read about the many smart girls out there who prove it's wrong. There's 13-year-old Julia Bluhm who convinced a US teen magazine not to digitally alter body sizes on its pages. Or Allyson Ahlstrom, a fashion philanthropist

definitions

{ DOUBLE STANDARDS }

'Rules' that are applied in different ways to different people. For instance, boys might be praised for dating lots of girls, while girls are criticized for dating lots of boys.

who at 15 started an initiative to give new, donated designer clothes to poor teens who would never be able to afford them. Or how about Marie Curie, the first woman to win a Nobel peace prize and the only woman to ever win two Nobel peace prizes? Or Amelia Earhart, the first female aviator to fly solo across the Atlantic Ocean? The list of women you can admire is endless!

girls and sport

By the age of 14, girls drop out of sports at twice the rate boys do.
WOMEN'S SPORTS FOUNDATION

This might sound like a strange question in a world dominated by female Olympic winners, athletes, boxers and tennis champions – but how sporty are you for a girl? It really shouldn't even be an issue and yet, sport is still dominated largely by men and boys. You may be good at gymnastics, but it's the traditionally male sports, like football, cricket, rugby and athletics, that receive most focus and attention and attract the highest salaries and kudos.

That's also why you'll most likely be able to name more famous sportsmen than women. And even when women are successful at sport, sections of the media treat them very differently to how they treat sportsmen. Rather than being rated on their skills or asked about their success and self-belief, female athletes such as Wimbledon Champion Marion Bartoli or Olympic swimmer Rebecca Adlington, are often rated on, or asked about, their looks, their clothes or their relationship status. As a girl you need to prove yourself on the physical front. This is not because girls aren't sporty, strong or fast, but because girls aren't always encouraged to excel in these areas by their friends, school or family.

> **"When you get to 13 sport is not the thing girls want to do, there are other things happening. Girls in my year didn't want to get hot and sweaty. It didn't appeal to them. Having a mentor is key to changing girls' attitudes. I got into sport at the age of 10. It changed me and made me who I am. I was quite shy and sport gave me confidence."**
>
> JESSICA ENNIS, OLYMPIC MEDAL WINNER

According to the UK's Women's Sport and Fitness Foundation, just 12% of 14-year-old girls do the recommended amount of physical activity. If you've backed away from being physical it may be time to consider why. Have you retreated from sport because…

✳ You're the last to be picked for teams?

✳ You feel sport is about popularity and humiliation?

✳ You feel uncomfortable having to run about in sports gear in front of everyone?

✳ **You hate looking sweaty or getting sweaty?**

✳ **You are too embarrassed to show your body?**

✳ **You have zero interest in sport as you think it's for boys?**

The reality is that a majority of girls hate and opt out of PE for all of the above reasons and more. However, being physically active is not just about winning or being picked for teams. Sport is good for a number of reasons. Health benefits aside, it's excellent for your self-esteem and body image, plus feeling strong physically can help you to feel strong emotionally.

The answer is not to retreat from sport and see it as something only 'for boys' but to find an activity that suits who you are. There are plenty of sports that are rewarding in their own right and not all are competitive or team sports. The trick is to find something you love whether it's martial arts, football, free running, skateboarding or canoeing – and do it just for you.

be the boss of you!

DOUBLE STANDARDS

Double standards are everywhere. They can apply to how boys are treated compared to girls and to how boys and girls are allowed and expected to behave, both at home and at school.

At home you might notice these double standards in the way girls and boys are treated. Some families don't expect boys to do as much housework as girls or they expect boys to be the ones who always have to help their dad.

Double standards are at work all around you. For instance, look at how singer Miley Cyrus and Justin Bieber are treated. Both are around the same age and both are trying to shed their 'kiddie' image by behaving in wild ways, but one is treated much more harshly than the other in the media. Is this fair?

Sometimes you might find these double standards are in your favour and other times they won't be. For instance, you might find that as a girl you're encouraged to play football or basketball, whereas a boy who wants to do ballet might be teased or discouraged. The problem with double standards is they don't do any of us any favours. They basically make us all feel as if we have to obey all the so-called rules of what's acceptable or be made to feel bad if we don't.

So what's a girl to do? Well you can start by refusing to play the double standards game yourself. Refuse to let others tell you what you can and can't do just because you're a girl. In a nutshell, be the boss of you!

When you are aware of the double standards at play in your life, challenge them when they bother you. Sometimes just saying why you feel something is unfair and acknowledging the situation out loud can feel enough. But you might be surprised to find that some people agree to make things fairer as soon as you point out the double standard to them.

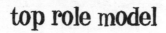

top role model

BETHANY HAMILTON SURFING CHAMPION

Surfer Bethany Hamilton has become a source of inspiration to millions of girls through her story of determination and hope in overcoming her personal and sporting setbacks. Bethany began surfing when she was very young and by the age of eight she entered her first surf competition, where she won both the short and long board divisions.

Then, on 31 October 2003, when she was 13 years old, Bethany was attacked by a 14-foot tiger shark while surfing off Kauai's North Shore. Bethany lost her left arm in the attack, but this didn't stop her. Just one month later, she returned to the water to continue pursuing her goal to become a professional surfer.

At the age of 14, Bethany made her return to competitive surfing, coming fifth in the Open Women's division. And, just over a year after losing her arm in the shark attack, she came first in the Explorer Women's division of the 2005 NSSA National Championships, winning her first national title.

Since then Bethany has become a pro-surfer and has won numerous awards for her charitable efforts and overall spirit. Bethany now has her own foundation, 'Friends of Bethany', which supports shark attack survivors, amputees, and serves to inspire others through her life story.

why sport is important for girls

Research from the World Health Organisation suggests two ways in which physical activities can contribute to better overall health in girls.

* There is evidence that regular physical activity can have a positive effect on your body image and psychological well-being. Studies show that girls respond more strongly to this than boys because they tend to start with lower self-esteem than boys.

* Research on physical activity also shows sport can help reduce levels of anxiety and depression. Further studies of female sports participation have also shown that they can contribute to a more generalised feeling of empowerment. This may be because participating boosts your self-esteem and being sporty carries with it a strong identity and self-direction.

how to be a body confident girl

*Two out of three
girls under 13 years
have already started dieting.

BLISS MAGAZINE

It's a real challenge to feel good about the way we look all the time in a world obsessed with unattainable ideals of beauty. As a girl perhaps you've been told you're too fat or too thin, or you're plump and need to be 'careful' or you're short or tall 'for a girl' or that you're 'apple-shaped' or 'pear-shaped' or need to eat more. There is even a range of made-up names, such as muffin tops, thigh gaps, bingo wings, back fat or cankles, which are used to describe girl's and women's body parts, and which add to the pressure!

The good news is that in a world that can feel as if it is trying to make you loathe your body and constantly strive for perfection, there are ways to feel both good about yourself and good enough. This chapter is all about improving your relationship with your body – how to like the way you look, 'own' your body and feel truly happy in your own skin.

female body criticism (and how to tackle it)

We are constantly bombarded with images of the ideal woman, on magazine covers, in newspapers and adverts, TV shows and films. This ideal woman is tall, slim and beautiful with perfect skin – but the truth is she doesn't even exist! Most of the images we see in the media have been retouched by computer software to give the illusion of perfection.

This vision of what the ideal woman should look like is the reason why diets are booming and why so many girls are overly critical about what they see in the mirror. It's also part of the reason why criticism about women's and girls' bodies is on the rise. Have you noticed, for example, that it has become acceptable to mention when a celebrity has put on a few pounds or left the house without make-up?

You may think that the media's obsession (and this includes social media) with celebrities' body flaws is just a bit of meaningless fun, but

> **"You have to say screw those people. I experienced it in school before I was famous. We see this airbrushed, perfect model and then if you don't look like that... You have to look past it – you look how you look, and be comfortable. What are you going to do? Be hungry every single day to make other people happy? That's just dumb."**
>
> JENNIFER LAWRENCE

this isn't the case. By making female body bashing seem like a normal and acceptable thing to do, we're saying it's okay for people to criticise everyone else for the way they look too.

If you don't believe this is true, consider how you think about your body.

* **Are you super-critical of your appearance when you look in the mirror?**

* **Do you ever wish you could radically change your body?**

* **Do you feel everything would be great in your life if your body was more perfect?**

how do we break the cycle?

Stop looking at female bodies critically. If you make fun of celebrity flaws, then you're saying it's ok for people to look at you and other girls and women that way too.

Stop looking at yourself so critically. Turn your focus away from your supposed 'flaws' and focus instead on your good points. Do this at least twice a day so it becomes a habit that you start to believe. Focus on what you love about yourself – whether it is your hair, your eyes or your hands and nails – and make the most of them!

the F-word

It's time to talk about the F-word. Fat. Are you conscious of your weight? Do you wish you had a flatter tummy, thinner thighs or a smaller bum? Do you avoid certain foods, skip meals or eat secretly because you're embarrassed about your weight? We live in a world that is overly focussed on female body weight. We're not talking about the health-threatening issue of real obesity, but on the pressure women face to be thin rather than healthy. Think of all the people you know who complain about their weight, or are on constant diets, or quote articles about celebs who've had plastic surgery or gastric bands?

Judging people because of their weight is all too common. How many times have you heard or seen the word 'fat' used as an insult or as something to laugh at? It's the reason why lots of girls can become obsessed with what they weigh and feel unhappy about their size, and this can be the reason why some of them focus their lives around what the weighing scales say instead of getting out there, having fun and living the life they want!

The problem with weight is that we are surrounded by hugely unrealistic and contradictory expectations of what girls' bodies should look like. These expectations make many of us believe that there is only one way to be a girl: slim and attractive. This is one reason why unrealistic sizes (such as 'size zero') persist and drive many girls to extreme dieting and self-hate.

"Girls of all kinds can be beautiful – from the thin, plus-sized, short, very tall, the quirky, the clumsy, shy, outgoing and all in between. ...Pledge that you will look in the mirror and find the unique beauty in you."

TYRA BANKS, MODEL, ACTRESS, TV PRESENTER

At a time when two-thirds of 13-year-olds are saying they are extremely worried about getting fat and, coupled with the fact that puberty is starting earlier (making girls more conscious of body and weight at 9 and 10 years rather than 11 and 12), it's about time we all got weight into perspective...

your family and food

Another factor worth thinking about is how your family talks about weight. If your parents make negative remarks about your body or their bodies, ban foods or comment on what you're eating, you're more likely to eat for comfort. Comfort eating is when you eat, not because you're hungry, but to feel better when you're upset or feeling down.

While being at a healthy weight (and this spectrum is larger than most people think) is good for your body and mind, constantly beating yourself up about your body size, fat and the way you look is a bad thing.

Confidence in yourself and your body doesn't come from a set of weighing scales but from what you do in life. This means how you feel about who you are inside and out, and what kind of person you are. Remember, you are more than your body weight, more than your clothes size and more than what you eat!

are you over-focused on weight?

Do you worry about your weight all day or is the word 'fat' not even on your radar? Find out with our quick quiz.

1 What is your first thought when you try on a cool pair of jeans in a shop?

    a Do they make me look fat?

    b Will my friends like these?

    c Do I like these enough to buy them?

2 If someone tells you that you have put on weight, is your first thought:

    a To feel angry. How dare they say that!

    b To feel ashamed and want to hide away

    c To feel embarrassed, but also annoyed at them?

3 A relative tells you that you shouldn't be eating cake as it makes you fat. Do you:

a Stop eating at the time but eat it in secret later
b Laugh it off but feel hurt
c Say nothing but eat some more just to make a point?

4 Do you feel your life would be brilliant if you were thinner?

a No
b Sometimes
c Always

5 When you see your reflection, do you:

a Quickly look away. You're not keen on seeing yourself in the mirror.
b Take a look – you need to fix something
c Glance at yourself quickly, but you're not that bothered?

scores

1 A 0   B 5   C 10
2 A 10 B 0   C 5
3 A 0   B 5   C 10
4 A 10 B 5   C 0
5 A 0   B 5   C 10

results

• •

0 – 15
You definitely worry too much about your weight and it's affecting your whole life. Do not feel ashamed about your body or your eating habits or wish yourself thinner. It's a waste of time and energy. Instead focus on feeling more positive about yourself and who you are (see page 50). You're worth it – you really are!

20 – 35
You're concerned about weight but you try not to let it rule your life. You're on the right track, just remind yourself that no one has the right to comment on your body or your eating habits or police your weight. You are in charge of your body and no one else. The ideal body is one that is happy and healthy, and not a particular shape!

40 – 50
You're not overly concerned about your weight or being fat and you like your body for what it is. Plus you know exactly how to handle criticism in this area. Go girl – you've got it sussed!

diets and eating disorders

Low self-esteem and negative messages about body size are one of the main reasons why the diet industry is booming. It's why diet books are on the bestseller lists every year and the diet industry makes millions. Yet, little attention is ever given to the reasons why so many people over-eat and eat for comfort.

The problem with diets is that they give you an unhealthy relationship with food.

definitions

{ EATING DISORDER }
a psychological illness characterized by abnormal and disturbed eating habits, such as not eating or overeating.

Making a conscious decision to swap unhealthy eating habits for healthy eating habits is one thing, but trying not to eat what you want and eating what someone else tells you to eat is something else entirely. It often works for a while, but it rarely teaches us to eat healthily or helps us to come to terms with healthy eating.

What's more, in a world dominated by celebrity figures, this also leads to a whole range of celebrity diets that encourage you to try every fad from the baby food diet, the fruit-only diet, the cabbage diet and much worse.

Then there are eating disorders. Currently, there are 300,000 teenagers in the UK who suffer from eating disorders such as anorexia, bulimia and overeating.

the big issue!

DIETS

Know the difference between healthy eating and dieting. One is about about eating a range of healthy food groups, plus a little of what you want, and the other is about restricting foods. And remember these points:

* In most cases dieting doesn't work because it doesn't teach you to eat healthily, only to deny yourself what you want.

* A healthy diet/eating plan is one that you should be able to adopt for life, not just something you do to lose weight before going back to your old habits.

* Don't make food the enemy. There are no good or bad foods, only foods that should be eaten in moderation in a healthy diet.

Research by the National Eating Disorder Collaboration has shown that eating disorders often start in the teenage years and are associated with cultural, social, behavioural and psychological factors. Eating disorders are, at their heart, a mental illness caused by deep-seated distress and unhappiness. They tend to occur when people focus on their body and eating habits as a way of trying to cope with other factors in their life. The repercussions are severe and can lead to being taken into hospital and a lifetime of health problems. If you suspect you have an eating disorder, see 'Be the change' section on page 126-127 for details on where to go for help and support.

mums, daughters and self-esteem

Only 2% of women feel comfortable describing themselves as beautiful.

DOVE UK

Negative ideas about your weight, body and looks can often be picked up from friends and family. So start to become aware of any throwaway comments your mum makes about her body and yours. Does she sigh when she looks in the mirror or say things like 'These jeans would look really nice on a thin person'? Does she critique your body in what she thinks is a 'helpful' way? Has she made you think that maybe you're not good enough the way you are? If so, it may be time to talk about these issues with her.

Mums mean well. Your mum is probably only trying to help you make the 'best of yourself' (as she sees it) and she probably doesn't mean to project her body issues on to you. But, if you feel under pressure from your mum about weight and dieting talk to her. Tell her how her comments are making you feel about yourself and see if together you can put an end to the 'fat talk'.

be the boss of you!

BE BODY HAPPY

Change the way you talk about yourself and to yourself!

1 Stop beating yourself up about not being perfect. Think about your health and fitness over and above your body weight and clothes size. What's important is that you eat healthily and stay active. That's the way to feel good about yourself and your body.

2 Get used to looking at your body as a whole. Look in a full-length mirror once a day and find five good things about yourself. This might

feel weird at first, but over time it will really boost your self-esteem.

3 Throw out the weighing scales or avoid getting on them. Weight fluctuates daily and scales do not give you an accurate picture of what you really look like.

4 Don't let other people comment on your weight. Adults can be bad at this too. You can close them down by telling them they are hurting your feelings.

5 Stop looking in the mirror all the time. Checking yourself out can become an excuse to constantly criticize yourself. Look when you need to, say something nice to yourself and then move on.

fashion and beauty

There are 3 billion women who don't look like supermodels and only 8 who do.

THE BODY SHOP

What's not to love about fashion and beauty? Pretty clothes, smiling models, great make-up and hair. It's fun. It's something to get lost in, plan to make a career out of or just follow because you get pleasure from it. However you feel about fashion and beauty, it's impossible not to ignore the impact these industries have upon body image and the way you feel about yourself as a girl.

The fashion and beauty industries are part of the reason many of us are so unhappy about how we look, but there is something you can do about it. For example, if fashion magazines make you feel inadequate, don't buy them. Fashion at its core is aspirational – it's meant to make us feel clothes and styling could transform us. It doesn't represent real women. In the end, the fashion and beauty industries are there to sell products.

By all means enjoy fashion and beauty, but don't get sucked into thinking that you need to look like the women in adverts. Too much emphasis on fashion and beauty (whether it's via magazines, reality shows or You Tube tutorials) can make you feel dissatisfied with your own body and make you want to change yourself with new clothes, faddy diets or lots of make-up.

In the end, it's simple. If the mags, ads, or images you're looking at make you feel bad, then cut down the amount of time you spend looking at them. You'll feel a whole lot better about yourself and you'll have a lot more fun if you spend that time on some other interests instead.

Also trying to look like a model is pointless. The rise in model TV shows and the culture of models as celebrities is just part of the unhealthy obsession with our bodies. So it's worth bearing in mind that girls only get chosen to be models because they don't conform to a norm. Most models are 5ft 10' and over, genetically

"When I started Rookie magazine, there were a lot of girls like me who had fashion blogs and loved getting dressed up and thinking about appearance, not in a stressful women's magazine way, but in a creative way. I can understand how some feminists who've fought against things like style or beauty defining all women might feel confused about how we can discuss self-esteem and being your own person, but also write so much about fashion. But I want there to be a place where women can do that, where you can care about fashion, and even be super girly, and it doesn't necessarily mean that you're not also smart or confident or strong."

TAVI GEVINSON, FASHIONSPOT

predisposed to look long and lean. Most of them look good because they are constantly groomed, styled and made-up by a team of professionals whose job it is to spend hours creating this look.

In most cases, models don't even look like the images you see of them. The photos we see are usually altered and improved by programs like Photoshop. We all know this happens, but did you know magazines do more than airbrush out the odd zit? They erase normal, rounded tummies, legs are stretched to look longer than normal, and the natural texture of skin (such as lines, freckles and pores) vanish. Some people believe alterations like these should be stopped, because of the pressure it puts on the rest of us to achieve impossible levels of perfection. What do you think?

None of this means you cannot be into fashion and beauty. By all means have fun with it, be a lipstick fiend, follow fashion magazines, and enjoy experimenting with clothes. But at the end of the day don't let fashion and beauty dictate the rules for what it means to be a girl.

brazilians and botox

Why as girls and women is there pressure to:

* Wax or otherwise remove our body hair – from legs, arms and underarms to the pubic area?

* Pluck, shape, tweak and groom our eyebrows into submission?

* Inject our faces and lips with Botox?

These questions and more are just some of the things you need to consider when you're a girl. Why are we surrounded by hype that suggests girls are supposed to look as plastic and hair-free as a Barbie doll? And why do girls have to work so hard to achieve this when everywhere you look there are guys with bushy eyebrows, body hair and wrinkles?

definitions

{ BOTOX }

A drug prepared from a toxin called botulin, used cosmetically to remove wrinkles by temporarily paralysing facial muscles.

The issue is, of course, that somehow over the course of time the idea has developed that body hair on women is unattractive. It's the reason why so many women put themselves through a variety of beauty 'tortures', such as having painful

continues on page 60

be the boss of you!

BODY PERFECTIONISM

If you've ever felt that cosmetic surgery might make you feel better about yourself, then bear the following things in mind:

1 Most women are self-conscious about their bodies and almost everyone wishes there were a thing or two that could be changed. Plastic surgery won't solve underlying problems – body image goes deeper than you think.

2 What you view (magazines, TV, film, YouTube) and who you hang around with have a huge effect on how you think you look and what you believe women should look like.

3 People who have very self-critical friends are likely to think that changing their looks will solve their problems. So think about who you are hanging around with and why.

4 If you're very focused on wanting cosmetic surgery then you need to talk to someone like your mum or someone else you trust about your body image.

5 Improving how you feel about yourself is key to learning to like yourself. Surround yourself with people who are positive about their bodies. Look for the positives in all kinds of body shapes and start listing all the positives about your body. Make being positive about yourself the norm and see what it does for your self-esteem.

injections in their foreheads and hot wax spread onto their intimate regions. It's also why, as females, we spend countless hours staring into the mirror and focusing on our perceived imperfections and worrying that our body hair is somehow overtaking our lives.

And while we all know it's ridiculous to load so much significance onto the perfect shape of our brows or the amount of hair we have on our arms, it can be hard to make a stand. That's why you need to give yourself a break. Looking at or thinking about your brows or hair on your legs too often is guaranteed to make you feel uncomfortable and self-conscious about it. Remind yourself that body hair is just body hair. It should not mean anything more than that.

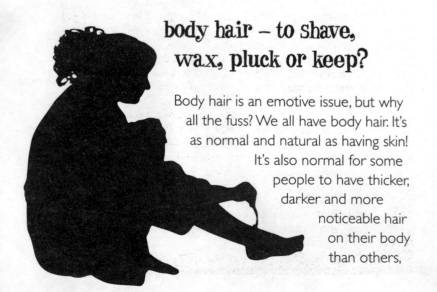

body hair – to shave, wax, pluck or keep?

Body hair is an emotive issue, but why all the fuss? We all have body hair. It's as normal and natural as having skin! It's also normal for some people to have thicker, darker and more noticeable hair on their body than others,

the big issue!

BOTOX AND COSMETIC SURGERY

Surveys show that there is an increasing trend for ever younger women to seek everything from botox to plastic surgery procedures. And while anti-ageing products used to be aimed at over-45s, now they are pitched at a younger market, with anti-ageing creams and products for women in their 20s. How long will it be before teens are asked to consider what they can do to stop the ageing process too?

If you think the world of plastic surgery and body perfection isn't touching you, think again. Much of the celebrity media that we see has a huge impact on what we start to believe is normal and acceptable in bodies and what isn't.

When these images make girls and women feel as if they are not good enough, plastic surgery can seem like an option to some. But the answer is not surgery to make you 'body perfect', but to remember that the images you see in media and adverts are altered in Photoshop to portray an unrealistic look.

Women on TV or films have specialist make-up artists at hand to make their skin and hair look flawless and everything from spots and freckles to scars and creases is hidden from view. To give yourself a wake-up call, look at the women you know around you – very few of us have perfect skin, bodies or perfect anything – because we're real. (By the way if you ever see a celebrity in the flesh you'll realise how 'real' they look too!)

just like people have head hair of different colours and thicknesses. Yet, having body hair has somehow become associated with not being feminine, hygienic or attractive.

Pubic hair in particular has come in for the most criticism. This is partly down to the recent craze for Brazilian and Hollywood waxes that have made the bikini line (your pubic hair region) a fashion statement. Thankfully, these types of beauty treatments have fallen out of favour of late, with many women realising that pubic hair isn't unhygienic and unattractive and doesn't need to be waxed away completely, if at all.

So what's a girl to do about body hair? Well, that's a individual thing and is up to each and every one of us. However, putting your body hair into perspective before you rush to get rid of it can help you to see how hard we are on our bodies and how much other people's opinions matter, when they shouldn't.

Having said that, like everything else, body hair removal is a personal choice. Some girls can't live with hairy armpits; others feel they need to wax or bleach the darker hairs on their top lip to feel at their very confident best. That's no problem, of course, but what's key here is not to be pulled into the myth that having body hair is 'anti-girl'. Body hair is simply just body hair, and like the hair on your head, you can grow it, limit it or just ignore it. The choice here is yours, and yours alone.

breasts and puberty

One of the reasons that the cosmetic surgery industry has boomed over the last 20 years is the endless focus in the media on women's figures, and in particular on their breasts. This media attention is why while having a boob job was once considered an extreme measure (and still is by many), today it is now much more common.

Images of women's breasts, whether they are shown topless in newspapers or commented on in websites and magazines, are an example of objectification. That's when women are portrayed in ways that suggest that they are just objects to be looked at, ogled, or even touched. It reduces women to anonymous objects to be looked at and admired, not as full human beings with equal rights and needs.

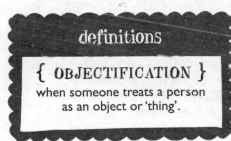

definitions

{ OBJECTIFICATION }
when someone treats a person
as an object or 'thing'.

Of course, we don't have to buy into this. We all know the truth is that your cup size doesn't define you or say anything about the kind of person you are. Beauty comes in all shapes and sizes and no matter what shape you are, breasts don't have the power to make you happy or unhappy; they're just another part of your body like your arms and legs.

top role model

TAVI GEVINSON FASHION BLOGGER

Tavi Gevinson has been writing her infamous fashion blog, *Style Rookie*, since she was 11 years old, posting her thoughts on fashion and reviews of runway shows to musings on being a girl. At the age 15 Tavi also created an online magazine called *Rookie*, a for-girls-by-girls platform for talking honestly, openly, and smartly about feminism and other issues unrelated to fashion.

Despite the criticism against her, which has some fashion editors and media critics, among others, saying that she has no business giving us her views, Tavi and *Rookie* have gone from strength to strength, breaking one-million page views within five days of launching in September 2011.

Tavi has sat in the front row at fashion shows, written about everything from Miley Cyrus (in *Elle* magazine) to going to your high school prom. She's even given a prestigious TED talk about how she had a hard time finding strong female teenage role models – so she built a space where they could find each other.

She also has two books out, is starring in a play on Broadway, is about to go to college and writes for several publications including *Harper's Bazaar, Jezebel, Lula, Pop*, and GARAGE magazine – proving she's one of the best teen girl role models around.

This is especially important during puberty when our bodies are changing shape. We all need to remind each other that it is normal and natural for breasts and other body parts to come in different shapes and sizes. There really isn't one ideal shape or size.

what is body confidence?

So what equals body confidence in a girl? If you ask a hundred people you will probably get a hundred different answers. What's important is not what everyone else thinks, but what YOU think.

Girls who are body confident can be any shape, size and weight. Some are brilliant at sports and some aren't. Some have a flair for fashion and others live in jeans and t-shirts. Others are loud and excitable and some are quiet and shy. They may have body worries, but they keep these fears in perspective by not allowing others to characterize them by their so-called 'flaws'.

Body confident girls are brave (because it's hard to stand up to criticism), smart (because why waste your life worrying about your clothes size?) and most of all they work hard to find the positives in themselves. After all, if you can spend all day obsessing over what's wrong with you, surely you can spend five minutes or more finding out what's right, too?

how to be a girl in relationships

*One in three 11–12 year olds (37%) say they have been in a boyfriend/girlfriend relationship.

The world of love and dating can have a lot going for it, when you're ready for it. It can be exciting and fun to flirt with guys, go on dates and fall in love, but there are some downsides to forming relationships. Like anything else, it pays to learn how to negotiate the world of dating from the word go!

The problem with being a girl and starting to date is that sometimes double standards and stereotyping can come into play. Alongside all the good stuff, you may find certain expectations placed on you. Some girls feel a pressure to behave and act in a certain way (such as more giggly and needy, less opinionated, flirtier than they really are or even something worse) in order to get a boy's attention.

These expectations don't necessarily come from boys (though sometimes they can), but they can come from the things that you and your friends believe, watch and read on social media, TV or films.

Having said all that, dating should be a fun not stressful or worrisome part of your life. If you're smart you can navigate your way through it, enjoying it for what it is – something to enjoy, something to make you happy and something not serious. Here's how to do it.

a girl's view of boys

"I love boy bands, they are the boys I like – good looking, clever and talented. Not the ones in my class who just act like little kids."

TIA, 13

What do you think about boys? Do you think they're amazing and too good to cast a look in your direction? Do you hold boys to a different standard than your friends? Do you expect boys to ask you out and suggest what you do and where you go? If so, watch out because you may be falling for some dating stereotypes!

In the same way that girls can feel pressure that boys want them to look and act a certain way, boys are under a similar pressure too. If you and your friends sit around discussing which boys are good looking and attractive and which aren't, then you're doing the same thing that some boys do to girls, i.e. you're judging boys simply on their looks.

Why do some of us have a pretty set idea about what boys are like and the way they should behave when they are with girls? Think about what your own views of boys are based on. Are they based on reality? Are they based on messages you've received from your family or friends, or truths that you've discovered for yourself? Are the things you watch and read, such as romantic novels or chick flicks, giving you an idealised view of boys and what you expect from them?

Only you can say how you really view boys, but bear in mind all these things can play a big part in the boyfriends you choose to date, what you put up with and the way you behave in your relationships.

what do boys want?

The popular idea of what boys want is to have sex with girls and then ditch them! They are supposedly obsessed with sex and totally uninterested in being faithful or nice. This is all a myth! The sex-starved teenage boy is just another popular stereotype that you see in the media and maybe even in your own life (some boys seem to feel they have to live up to this idea)!

The truth is that most boys basically want the same things as you. When they are ready they want someone who likes them, cares about them and wants to go out with them. They are just as afraid of being rejected (worth bearing in mind when someone asks you out), they're just as confused about sex and they feel under pressure to act like the kind of boy they are led to believe that girls want. Basically, boys are often also confused and scared about girls.

What's more, they are as much at the mercy of images of perfection as the rest of us and worry about their bodies not being good enough, not being good looking enough, tall enough, muscly enough and more. So don't fall into the trap of thinking that they need to be put on a pedestal or put down. Boys are just like you, negotiating their way through puberty and growing up!

A recent survey of teen boys found that they are motivated more by love and a desire to form real relationships than some people seem to think. A report from New York State University found that 80% of boys said being physically attracted to someone wasn't the primary motivation for dating a girl, but really liking them and wanting to get to know someone better was the main reason.

All of this is important to know as a girl because it stops you from believing that boys are so different to girls. If you realise that they also have fears and anxieties about sex and falling in love, it will help you to feel more relaxed. If you accept that they also have insecurities and worries about not being good enough, then it enables you to see them in a more realistic light. What's more, realising that it's harder for boys to show their feelings (as they tend to be ridiculed and bullied if they do) can also help you to understand why boys tend to talk less about how they feel and why they sometimes behave the way they do.

> **"Mutual respect is one of the most important foundations for a strong, healthy relationship. Respect means seeing each other as equals, treating them with dignity–even in conflict, empathizing with their needs, trusting them, and giving validation. This should be afforded to both partners."**
>
> LACI GREEN, POSITIVE SEX AND RELATIONSHIPS CAMPAIGNER.

being in a relationship

Whether you have a boyfriend, want a boyfriend or are wondering what it'd be like to have a boyfriend, it's worth knowing the effect love and relationships can have on you as a girl. The problem with being in a relationship with someone is that while it can make you feel amazing, it can also make you feel confused or even terrible. If you've chosen someone smart and mature who cares about you, then it will be a positive thing. However, if you've unknowingly chosen someone who lacks maturity (because it's not always easy to see what someone is really like at first), this isn't such a great thing as they can play silly relationship games that leave you feeling vulnerable or make you feel as if you need to change who you are, just to please them.

As we've seen, boys have their own issues going on and their own pressures forcing them to behave in

the big issue!

ONLINE PORN

At some point in your life you may have glimpsed porn on YouTube, Tumblr, Vine – or viewed something you'd rather not have that was sent to you as a joke on Facebook, What's App or Snapchat.

It's normal to be curious about sex and sexuality when you're young, but it's really important to realise that pornography does not give a realistic view of the way real men and women look or how they behave in a sexual relationship. Just as with the photo-shopped images we see in magazines, bodies shown in porn are edited so they look more 'perfect' than real bodies and real sex isn't like staged pornographic sex either.

The reason porn is worth mentioning in this chapter is that it can distort a few people's ideas of what bodies should look like and what a sexual relationship is like. However, thankfully on the whole most people do understand that porn is like the car chase scenes in action movies – it's exciting to watch, but not the way to drive.

certain ways, but one of the main pressures on them comes from their peers – other boys. This means some boys tend to be at the mercy of their mates. This can lead to a number of things when you start dating or liking a boy. For example, some boys might…

* Tell their friends more than they need to know about you.

* Brag or possibly even lie about what happens within your relationship.

* Allow their friends to influence decisions about your relationship (something girls do as well), such as seeing you less than he wants to or ignoring you when his mates are around.

So, how do you deal with boys? It's simple: communicate and listen. This means being honest and clear with them in the way you would with your friends. Don't imagine they are all after one thing, or different to you, or that all they want is a string of girlfriends. Don't read things into what they say and do. If they're ignoring you, it's not because they secretly like you, and if they flirt with your friends it isn't to make you like them!

What's more, even if a boy is your boyfriend, never ever let him tell you what to wear, who to be friends with or that you need to change some aspect of yourself. Relationships are about having fun. If you're not having fun, then you need to get out of that relationship fast.

are you falling for dating stereotypes?

Are you falling for dating stereotypes and myths? Try this fun quiz to find out.

1 When talking to a boy you like, are you...

    a Totally yourself

    b Giggly and self-conscious

    c Nervous and anxious?

2 Being single is a sign that...

    a No one wants to be with you

    b You simply haven't met the right person yet

    c You don't really want a boyfriend at the moment?

3 Your boyfriend ditches you for no reason and won't say why. What is your first thought?

   a What did I do wrong?
   b How can I get him back?
   c It's a good thing I found out that he wasn't right for me. Now I'm free to meet someone who is?

4 Your boyfriend flirts with your friend, it's a sign that…

   a He can't be trusted and doesn't respect your relationship
   b You need a new friend
   c He loves you?

5 You never get the boy you want because…

   a You don't look the way they want you to look
   b You're too loud
   c You haven't met the right one yet?

scores

1   A 10   B 0   C 5
2   A 0   B 5 ·   C 10
3   A 0   B 5   C 10
4   A 10   B 5   C 0
5   A 0   B 5   C 10

results

• •

0 – 15 *You're falling for the romantic myth that boys who like you play hard to get (they don't) and that boys like girls who are pathetic and weak. Successful dating calls for you to be yourself. That way you don't have to pretend all the time and you end up with someone who generally makes you happy!*

20 – 35 *You're a romantic at heart. Though you know logically that you should be yourself, you're also swayed by the idea that bad boys are nice really and that girls have to behave a certain way in relationships. Trust your gut instincts and be true to yourself!*

40 – 50 *You're no dating pushover. You know that finding the right relationship is all about being yourself, being honest and not dating just for the sake of it. Take your time to find the right boy.*

boyfriend expectations

When it comes to falling in love we all have ideas about what it will eventually mean and what it will do for us. Maybe you're a romantic who believes that your soul mate – the perfect boy for you – is out there somewhere. Or perhaps you believe that when you get a boyfriend all your problems will disappear and you'll never be unhappy again.

The truth is that while a good relationship is a fun and amazing thing, sometimes getting a boyfriend can mean getting all their problems too. What's more, if you expect a boyfriend to 'save you' in some way you're in for a big surprise. Getting a boyfriend may make you feel wanted and approved of for a bit, but it doesn't solve anything. You can feel good about yourself, feel worthy and be happy, without a boyfriend.

 You don't need a boyfriend to feel good about yourself. In the world of romantic films and books the 'loser' girl is always transformed by love (*Twilight* is a good example of this). In reality, being in a relationship won't change how you feel about yourself. If you feel unworthy, not pretty enough or not good enough, being asked out won't change this. It may make you feel better for a while, but being in a relationship when you feel like this can also make you needy and fearful of being left. The key to feeling better about yourself is not dating, but boosting your confidence and self-esteem by realising that you're not the inadequate or unlikeable person you think you are.

You don't need a boyfriend to feel worthy. Many people take having a boyfriend as a sign that they are lovable and worthy. Why? Well, some people seem to think that being chosen by a boy is a signal to the world that you're worth being chosen. The truth is we're all lovable and worthy without being someone's girlfriend. Think of all your friends who love you, all of the people in your family who care about you and the many reasons why you're a good person. You are brilliant with or without a boyfriend.

✱ **You don't need a boyfriend to be happy.** Do girls in relationships have more fun than single girls? No they don't. Ask any older girl or woman you know and you'll see that being in a relationship has no bearing on how happy you can be. Why? Well because happiness should never be dependent on one person and certainly not on your dating status.

The fact that you can be happy, feel worthy and feel good about yourself without a boyfriend in tow doesn't mean giving up on relationships. The right relationship can bring love, wonder, and much enjoyment if you date someone you like and respect, if you are honest and open when you're with them and if you take what you have together for what it is (not what you think a relationship should be).

the art of being happy – single or not!

It can be great to fall in love when the right boy comes along, but it is a waste of effort and energy to spend too much time thinking and talking about it until that happens. There's a lot of pressure on girls to be 'boy crazy' and it can be hard to avoid falling into this trap.

But wanting a boyfriend, searching for one or talking about getting one is not something you have to do all the time just because you're a girl. It's absolutely fine not to be interested in relationships. Yes, you may feel a little left out sometimes when friends start talking about it or when your best friends gets asked out on a date, but it's always better to be true to yourself.

> **"Independence comes from knowing who you are and being happy with yourself."**
>
> BEYONCÉ, SINGER

What's more, it's smart to realise from the beginning that not being interested in dating is a choice. It certainly doesn't mean that you're unattractive or dull or that you're deficient in some way. It simply means that you haven't met someone who makes you feel interested in doing so yet..

Plus, being on your own until you choose not to be has lots of advantages such as:

★ **There's no drama in your life**

★ **You don't have to worry about someone else's feelings and needs**

★ **You can do whatever you want to do when you want to do it**

★ **You can flirt with anyone you want (if you want to that is)**

★ **You can focus on all the other areas of your life that are every bit as important.**

dating double standards

We talked about double standards in chapter one, but double standards are scattered all over the dating world, too. In fact, there are possibly as many double standards for boys as there are for girls in the dating world. For instance, as you get older you might find that single boys are viewed in a different way than single girls or that some boyfriends think they should be able to make decisions for you.

What you have to remember is that unfair dating double standards like the ones above persist because we let them. Have you ever asked yourself why so many people seem to think girls shouldn't ask boys out or why boys should pay for dates because they're boys? In fact, many girls can and do ask boys out. And why should boys always be expected to pay for dates?

How should you handle the dating double standards? Well every time you feel one come your way, question it. For instance:

* **Why shouldn't girls ask boys out? What's so bad about being honest and proactive when you like someone?**

* **Why do boys have to pay for things? You're in the same financial boat so you should split things.**

* **Why should one person make all the decisions in a relationship? A good relationship is based on both of you making decisions.**

the let's-be-mean relationship game

Another relationship pitfall to watch out for is the lets-be-mean game. Being mean about people's dating behaviour and relationship choices can become an unpleasant habit that people easily fall into. Magazines and reality shows started this by publicly making fun of people for their relationship problems (the *Twilight* stars and Miley Cyrus for example) and their crazy behaviour when they are heartbroken. This kind of mean behaviour has filtered down to how some people behave online and to each other.

Think of the selfie meanness that goes on via Instagram, Ask or What's App when someone posts a picture of themselves with someone they like. Or the way we're all too happy to comment on someone's relationship status update. Or even the way we choose to talk meanly about a celebrity who dares to date more than one guy.

a key to the world of dating

When you get a bit older dating can be complicated, especially when you're not sure where you stand. At one time, you were either going out with someone or you weren't. Now, you can be seeing someone but they or you may be seeing other people too, or you may be seeing someone but on a break, which means you're together but not really together...

If this book teaches you anything it's that when you're ready to date, YOU make the decisions about your dating life. Not your friends and not your boyfriend. So never feel as if you have to stand in line waiting to be picked, or waiting for someone to decide if you're 100% together or not.

be the boss of you!

WHAT TO DO ABOUT MEAN BEHAVIOUR

1 Refuse to play the 'mean game' by not getting involved if and when friends do it. Just one person doing it makes everyone else think it's okay as it's just 'a bit of fun'.

2 If someone is mean, counteract it by being nice. Nothing stops mean comments faster than a nice one.

3 Don't watch shows that focus on being mean to people. *Fashion Police* and *Next Top Model* are good examples. Instead, watch the shows that make you feel good.

4 Avoid the apps and social media where mean behaviour is rife such as Ask.com and Tumblr. If you refuse to view it you won't feel as if mean behaviour is the norm.

5 Don't 'celebrity shame'. For example, playing the game that many tabloid newspapers and magazines participate in of being hyper-critical of a celebrity who is seen without make-up, has put on a bit of weight, or has been spotted with different 'partners'. Again it seems like a bit of fun to 'celeb shame', but it filters into real life!

6 If it ever happens to you don't just ignore it. Tell whoever is doing it that it hurts your feelings and you want them to stop. Then take action to ensure others know what's going on, by telling parents, other family members or teachers. Then make sure you take further action to avoid it, for instance by getting off social media if it's happening there or keeping out of the way of any so-called 'friends' who are doing it.

The basic rule of dating is that it should feel fun and make you feel good. It should be on your terms and you should set the agenda. That includes choosing if and when you are ready for a physical relationship. If it doesn't feel good and right, then you're better off being on your own until the right boy comes along.

a word about sex and relationships education

In England, Scotland, Northern Ireland and Wales people have to be 16 or older to have sex.

Sex and relationships education (SRE) is about more than biology and sex and it's vital if you want a healthy view of relationships. The right kind of sex and relationships education will tell you everything from how to handle peer pressure to consent and more.

You should get SRE in school from the age of 10+ however, only certain areas of SRE are statutory such as the biological aspects of human growth and reproduction that are essential elements of the national curriculum in science. This means you may not get all the information you need, which is why you owe it to yourself to go to a reputable SRE site (see 'Be the change' on pages 126-127) and find out what you need to know.

top role model :

YAS NECATI SEX EDUCATION CAMPAIGNER

Yas Necati is a 17-year-old blogger and activist and a proud member of 'No More Page 3', a campaign group fighting to end the portrayal of topless women in the Sun newspaper. She is also a passionate believer in better education, particularly regarding sex and relationships.

In January 2014, Yas won a petition launched alongside the *Telegraph* newspaper for better sex education in schools. The campaign was started by Yas and 15-year-olds Georgia Luckhurst and Lili Evans who all felt that the current curriculum lets down young people when it comes to sex and relationships guidance in the real world.

Yas says she left school feeling uninformed and unprepared. 'It's all very well talking about biology, but when you get into a relationship, it's about so much more than just the science. Where is our guidance on that?' Yas says she felt let down and it upset her so much that she became really passionate about making a change so that other generations didn't have to go through such a poor and uninformative curriculum.

Her petition now has over 31,000 signatures and is growing every day. As well as this, she is part of the ongoing Campaign4Consent, looking to put sexual consent onto the national curriculum. Yas is a writer for the online movement SPARK and editor of Powered By Girl, an activist organisation looking to give young women opportunities in feminist writing.

how to be a
'good enough' girl

*During the last 10 years spending by teen girls on beauty products has risen by 90%.

MINTEL 2013

How important is it for you to be seen as perfect by others? Ask your friends what being perfect means to them and you might hear replies like a particular dress size, great exam results or just being an A-grade student. Or maybe all of these together!

The pursuit of perfection is a new level in the game of being a girl. Striving to be good, better or brilliant isn't necessarily a bad sort of pressure to put yourself under. In many cases, wanting to do better can help you by driving you to work hard at school, be a better friend or like yourself that bit more.

But if you can't tolerate making the slightest mistake, if you constantly focus on negatives and try to eliminate each and every one of them, or if you set your goals so high that you almost feel you will never reach them, then you've got a bad case of the perfectionism bug, and that's not so good.

The thing we all need to remember is that perfection doesn't exist, but being good enough does! Being good enough is an idea that starts in your mind (not on the scales or in the mirror) and grows from there. It's about knowing you're good enough just the way you are and that doing your best is more important than striving for unattainable perfection.

be the boss of you!

HOW TO FEEL 'GOOD ENOUGH' EVERY DAY

So how's a girl to feel good enough about herself every day? Well, one good way is to surround yourself with inspiring and uplifting quotes that 'speak' to you. It may sound corny but having inspiring words around you works wonders on your mind and can really give you a boost when you're feeling low or lacking in confidence.

You could make a mood board on your bedroom wall, using a pin board that has lots of pictures, quotes and things that make you feel good. Or you could just stick quotes where you can see them every day. Just saying these messages to yourself (known as mantras) can really pick you up when you feel down. The online site Pinterest (www.pinterest.com) is a brilliant place to find inspiring, girl- empowering mantras. Here are some powerful examples. Try to memorise a few and say them to yourself every day!

* Who I am is more than good enough.

* I am strong, I am brave and I am unstoppable.

* Real girls aren't perfect. Perfect girls aren't real.

* I am powerful and I am loved.

* I am positive and I am happy in my own skin!

* Why should I need to fit in, when I was born to stand out?

are you trying to be too perfect?

Are your goals realistic or do you think you need to strive to be perfect? Find out here!

1 How long do you spend getting ready before you go to school?

   a Half an hour or more – you have to do your hair and make-up

   b Ten minutes – you get dressed, eat and go

   c Twenty minutes – but you do your make-up on the way to school.

2 You get an answer wrong in class, what happens next?

   a You shrug it off but feel really embarrassed

   b You get upset and replay it over and over in your head at home

   c Shrug it off – it's not the end of the world?

3 A boy you really like sees you walking your dog in your scruffiest clothes. How do you act?

   a You don't care. This is you – and you dress as you like!

   b You make loads of excuses to him

   c Run and hide?

4 What's more likely to ruin your day: having bad hair, saying something silly in front of friends or getting a bad mark on a test?

   a Bad hair day definitely – you hate looking bad

   b None of that – you don't care about stuff like that

   c All of them – it's embarrassing to look bad and to lose face?

5 You see a picture of someone you really admire looking less than perfect. Does it put you off them?

   a A little – you don't like your heroes to look real

   b Yes – it's totally ruined how you thought of them

   c Not at all, that would be silly?

scores

1 A 0   B 10   C 5
2 A 5   B 0   C 10
3 A 10   B 5   C 0
4 A 5   B 10   C 0
5 A 5   B 0   C 10

results

●●●

0 – 15 You're eager to be perfect and as a result you have strict standards for you and everyone else around you. You need to see the quest for perfection is a waste of effort and that life will be much happier (and easier) if you relax, stop being so hard on yourself and just be yourself.

20 – 35 You would like to be perfect and feel embarrassed and ashamed when you don't meet the mark. Try to see that making mistakes, looking untidy and saying the wrong things is 100% normal (watch the blooper reels on films and TV to see this is true). No one is judging you so relax and have fun being you.

40 – 50 You couldn't care less about being perfect for yourself or for the sake of others. In fact you have a very healthy attitude to perfection. On some levels you want to strive to be better but on others you are happy as you are. Well done you!

how to take the focus off being perfect

As we've seen, the pressure to be 'perfect' can have a huge effect on your stress levels. You may have felt it during SATs in year 6, or with the start of secondary school. Perhaps everyone around you is freaking out about exams and what levels they are at. Wherever you are on the perfect student/girl scale here's what you need to know.

 You are more than your grades.
Yes, you want good marks and to do well in life but exams don't tell the whole story about you. Lots of people in life do amazingly well without being a star student or A-grade pupil at school. This is because tests don't measure things like creativity, emotional intelligence (your people skills), or entrepreneurial skills. So what's important is not to be a perfect student but to do your best, because in the end that's what counts the most.

✱ **Focus on how far you have come, not how far you have to go.** It's very easy with schoolwork to think of all the things you can't do or that you have got to do and to forget all that you've already done. Next time you feel your confidence flagging, give yourself a pep talk and remind yourself of all that you have achieved.

✱ **Have a life and interests away from school.** Focus on being a well-rounded person who has a life and interests away from school work too. Aside from the fact this is better for your self-esteem and stress levels, it's what colleges and work places look for when you apply for jobs and courses.

the power of positive role models

Role models are women (and men) we look up to. The best role model is someone you admire for a range of reasons. Someone who motivates you to do something, see something and try something. Having positive role models boosts your motivation and inspires you to reach your own goals.

Some role models are those who focus on important goals, such as helping a cause, helping others (see Top

Role Model Malala Yousafzei on page 102) or achieving something. Angelina Jolie combines her work as an actress with being a human rights activist and Camila Batmanghelidjh is famous for setting up the charity Kids' Company to support vulnerable inner-city children.

Other role models are inspiring because they overcome obstacles and show you that success is possible if you believe in yourself. People like Bethany Hamilton the surfing champion (see page 36), Paralympic gold medal-winning swimmer Ellie Simmonds MBE or J K Rowling, who came up with the *Harry Potter* stories while struggling to support her child and herself on welfare.

> **"Courage doesn't mean you don't get afraid. Courage means you don't let the fear stop you."**
>
> BETHANY HAMILTON, SURFER

The online world is a great place to find a role model and get inspired and even feel more hopeful about being a girl. There are heaps of teen activists trying to change the issues they feel strongly about. Take Jules Spector, 13, who has become a prominent voice in the feminist movement, founding the popular and influential blog Teen Feminist (see 'Be the change' on page 126-127), which serves as a platform for a broad spectrum of girl issues.

Then there are the girl sites that just beg to be visited for their huge range of role models. Try *The Mighty Girl* – the world's largest collection of books, movies, and music for smart, confident and courageous girls! Or *Love*

top role model

MALALA YOUSAFAZAI
FEMINIST CAMPAIGNER

Malala Yousafzai is an education activist from Pakistan. She is known for her peaceful activism for education rights for women especially in the Swat Valley, Pakistan, where girls had been banned from attending school. In early 2009, at the age of 11, she started writing a blog for the BBC detailing her life under Taliban rule, and her views on promoting education for girls.

On the morning of Tuesday 9 October 2012, Malala boarded a school bus in the northwest Pakistani district of Swat and a gunman got on, asked for her by name, then shot her three times. This sparked a national and international outpouring of support for Malala. So big is the level of support for her campaign that United Nations Special Envoy for Global Education Gordon Brown launched a petition using the slogan 'I am Malala', demanding that all children worldwide be in school by the end of 2015. This petition helped to bring about Pakistan's first Right to Education Bill.

In 2013, Malala spoke at the UN to call for worldwide access to education. Her amazing impact on the world current political events shows that one voice, even that of a young girl from a very poor country, can have a huge impact on raising awareness and encouraging change across the world.

Is Louder – a charity that supports anyone feeling mistreated, misunderstood or alone. It hears the voices of hundreds of thousands of girls just like you who have turned this idea into a whole movement.

friends don't need to be perfect

Friends and peers have a big influence on us. They are the ones who seem to set the rules. They can boost us up, but they can also knock us down – which is why perfectionism and friendship are often linked. Are your friends supportive? The people who understand you the most? The go-to people when you feel sad and anxious? Or do they expect you (and themselves) to be perfect and always go on about their (and your) failings? If that's the case, you need to have a long hard look at the standards you're holding each other too.

If you and your friends spend time hating the way you look and feeding your anxieties with endless selfies then that's going to be a problem in your life. Peer pressure from friends can also make life challenging in a number of other ways. For instance, you may feel pulled to act a certain way to be friends with a particular group. Or you may feel you have to go along with something just because everyone else is doing so.

The way to combat all of this is to be assertive. Assertiveness is a way of behaving that communicates what you think in a confident and non-threatening way. It's about standing firm in what you believe, such as the way you treat other people, and standing up for yourself with friends when they are pushing you in a direction you don't want to go in.

definitions

{ **ASSERTIVE** }
confident and direct when stating one's rights and views.

self-esteem is the key to feeling 'good enough'

If you want to believe in yourself and not hold yourself to unrealistic standards, you need to boost your self-esteem. Good self-esteem comes from having a sense of belonging, believing that you are capable, and knowing that you are valued by others for more than your looks and test results. It sounds like a big job, but really it isn't.

There are two types of people in particular who may need to work on their self-esteem:

1 **The people pleaser** People pleasers try to make everyone happy in their life by putting their needs second to others' needs. While it's good to care about your friends and family and want to help them and be there for them, don't do it at the expense of your sense of self.

2 **The human chameleon** While we all sometimes change ourselves a little to fit a situation, changing yourself into something you think others want you to be (i.e. the fun friend, the good daughter, the quiet girl) is a road to low self-esteem. Labels can trap us into roles, making it harder for us to become the person we really want to be!

The first step in improving your self-esteem is to look at your core beliefs about yourself. These are the deep beliefs you hold about yourself and your abilities. They could include things like believing you'll never be funny, smart or good at maths. Many core beliefs like this are things that you thought or someone said a long time ago and they just sort of stuck. They are not always right. Maybe you've simply forgotten to check whether or not they are true.

You can change your core beliefs by challenging yourself. This means changing your internal dialogue. (That is the voice in your head that says negative things to you sometimes!) Make it a voice that ups your confidence, makes you feel like you have a fan club inside your head and spurs you on in a proactive way. Say nice supportive things to yourself (as if you were talking to your best mate). And if you believe you're not smart or worthy, think of five smart things you're proud of – such as how you handled a situation with friends, when you got a grade you were proud of or when someone gave you a compliment.

definitions

{ SEXISM }
prejudice, stereotyping or discrimination, usually against women.

While you're at it, don't worry about what people think of you! Most of the time, the truth is they are looking too closely at themselves to be bothered about you. Try not to be too self-conscious or afraid that people will judge you harshly. Who cares what strangers think? Who cares what someone says about how girls should behave to be liked and respected? You get to make those decisions, not strangers, not your friends, after all it's your life!

Finally, when you're very down about yourself, let the adults in your life help you. School work, friends, secret worries, exams, extra-curricular classes, sports are not so important that you should let them make you anxious and stressed. While it's great that you don't want to

the big issue!

TEEN GIRLS AND SELF-HARM

You may not have come across the term self-harm but it's something that you might hear about in years to come. Self-harm is when someone hurts themselves to cope with their feelings and frustrations. Self-harm can range from scratching arms or pulling out hair to something even more serious. It is linked to low self-esteem, perfectionism and depression, and sufferers feel they are unable to ask for help so they suffer in silence. But there is no need to suffer as there is help available. If you self-harm, feel tempted to self-harm or know someone who self-harms, see 'Be the change' on page 126-127 for information on where to go for help.

let anyone down, it's also important to be completely honest about your feelings.

That means being honest with parents and teachers and telling them when you feel a pressure overload. You are more likely to get the help you need if you can be clear about why you feel under pressure and how you can't cope. Remember, no one expects you to be perfect, least of all the people who love you.

be the boss of you!

BIG YOURSELF UP!

The key aspect to having healthy girl friendships and not being drawn into the mean behaviour is to big up your confidence! Improving the way you feel about yourself makes you feel strong and empowered and here's the way to do it.

1 Speak nicely to yourself! Being nice to yourself is key to how you behave with others. If you are constantly critical of yourself and harsh and unrelenting when you make mistakes, then you're more likely to treat others this way too. Snap yourself out of it by saying three nice things to yourself daily. It's cringe-making at first but it works and will change your mindset.

2 Don't compare yourself with others. There will always be those girls who are prettier and more popular than you, in the same way that there will be girls who are less popular and less attractive, so what's the point in playing this game? Forget what everyone else is doing and focus on yourself. If you're happy, good enough and pleased with who you are, then you're winning!

3 Be honest about your feelings with friends and you'll be amazed at how many of them have exactly the same worries as you do – and how empowering it is not to feel you have to pretend all the time. Plus, you'll be reassured that people *like* you for who you really are and this in turn will make you feel strong and confident.

4 Accept others for who they are. Aside from the fact friends don't have to look like you, act like you and dress like you to be friends, accepting others for who they are (even when they are very different) is empowering. It shows the world you aren't afraid to make a stand for the things you like and love.

how to be a girl with a voice!

*Around the world women hold just 20% of seats in parliament.

THE ECONOMIST

Finding your 'voice' is all about finding your confidence. This is essential for many reasons, but one of the main ones is that in life you can come up against things that you need to speak out about. Being quiet, as opposed to loud and demanding, is a trait that is often encouraged in girls, but you can challenge this idea and this chapter is all about helping you to do that.

Why do you need a voice? Well, if you've ever witnessed double standards at play and thought it was unfair that boys are allowed to do something that girls aren't, or been upset at some sort of injustice (either personal or public), then you need a voice. Having a voice means having the courage to stand up for yourself and what you believe in. It's about believing that we are all equal and therefore should be held to the same 'rules'. It's about making sure that as a girl you have the same opportunities in life as a boy and being able to take action if someone is behaving badly towards you.

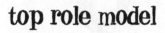

top role model

LAURA BATES WRITER & JOURNALIST

In April 2012, writer and journalist Laura Bates started a website called *Everyday Sexism* where women and girls could upload instances of sexism that they experience on a day to day basis. Some of the examples are serious, some are more minor, but they all catalogue things that have made women feel embarrassed, scared or annoyed.

Without any funding or means to publicise the project beyond her Facebook wall, she thought that perhaps 50 or 60 girls and women would add their stories. Within a week, hundreds had added their voices. Stories began to appear from America and Canada, Germany and France, Saudi Arabia and Pakistan, and tens of thousands of people started viewing the website each month.

Within 18 months the site had expanded to 18 countries. By December 2013, 50,000 entries had been uploaded to the site.

Laura's aim is to help girls and women to be aware of the possibility that things could be different for them through a change in ideas and assumptions about body image, and our 'everyday' behaviours towards each other. This was recently proven by her latest win when she invited her 143,000 followers on Twitter to let iTunes know that they didn't think it should be selling a plastic surgery app to nine-year-old girls. Within hours it had been withdrawn from sale. Now that's girl power!

how loud is your voice?

A voice is a powerful thing. Why not try this quiz to see how loud your voice is now?

1 A new school policy tells you what you can and can't do with your time at lunchtime. You think it's unfair – what do you do?

   a Take your case straight to the head teacher

   b Nothing – you don't want to get in trouble

   c Complain loudly about it with your friends?

2 How many causes do you feel passionate about?

   a None really – you haven't really thought about it

   b A couple – but you don't do much about it

   c One specific one – such as animal rights – and you're doing stuff to raise money and awareness?

3 You want to complain about how a teacher is treating you. What do you do?

a Nothing – who'd listen to you

b Take it up with your head teacher

c Tell your parents?

4 What makes you feel really angry?

a When you see an injustice against someone innocent

b When your parents say you can't go out with friends

c When you get into trouble at school and it's not your fault?

5 You feel strongly about what's happening to girls in other countries and want to raise money. How would you get your friends' support?

a You have no idea

b Go to the charity and ask how you can help

c Start a petition on social media?

scores

1 A 10 B 0 C 5
2 A 0 B 5 C 10
3 A 0 B 10 C 5
4 A 10 B 0 C 5
5 A 0 B 10 C 5

results

0 – 15 *Somewhere inside you is a voice that wants to get louder, it's just that right now you're not sure what you feel strongly about. Take the time to find causes that you believe in and feel you want to speak out for. It can be anything from why girls have to wear skirts instead of trousers at school to speaking out against bitching and bullying. Anything that helps you to realise your voice can make a difference.*

20 – 35 *You know what you feel passionate about and what makes you angry, but you're not always sure where to aim your voice. Just remember that being vocal about issues doesn't have to mean going global or big. Telling friends, drumming up support locally or going to the source of the problem works just as well.*

40 – 50 *You have a strong voice and strong beliefs and you know just where to go to make that voice heard, whether it's to your head teacher, the local paper or across social media. Well done you!*

why your voice is important

It's important to find your own voice: to know what you want to say and have the confidence to say it. This can be harder for girls than boys because they may not see so many women speaking out and getting things done in the world around them. This might be the case, for example, if you come from a very traditional culture or family and you receive very strong messages about male and female roles, but it's also true of politics and the media. Currently, less than a fifth of UK MPs are female, which means the main decision makers in the country are men. Women and girls represent half of the population but most of the people in power are male, and they may not always be the best choice to represent what females want and need.

> "I wanted to start a website for teen girls that was not kind of this one-dimensional strong character empowerment thing, because one thing that can be very alienating about a misconception of feminism is that girls then think that to be feminists, they have to live up to being perfectly consistent in their beliefs, never being insecure, never having doubts, having all the answers... and this is not true. Feminism is not a rule book but a discussion, a conversation, a process."
>
> TAVI GEVINSON FROM TED TALKS

What has all this got to do with you? Well, quite a lot really. At some point as a girl you're going to need to be able to say what you think and want. This might simply be to stop someone putting you down, to put yourself forward for a position as captain of a team or to join a school council, or it may even be to see how your voice can make a change in the world.

A brilliant way to start finding your voice is to follow women on social media who are great at speaking out on the topics that mean something to you. Girls and women are speaking out on topics all over social media. Also watch women you admire on YouTube and Ted (the 'Ideas Worth Spreading' site has a youth section – http:// www.ted.com/topics/youth).

Watching others speak up (even if they're not young and/or female) is one of the most powerful ways to get inspired and realise that your voice has power, no matter what your age or sex or nationality or religion!

sexual harassment and speaking up

One area in life in which girls need to know they have a voice if they need it is in the area of sexual harassment. Sexual harassment includes horrible things like being shouted at on the street by men and boys, teasing or off-hand remarks that make you feel uncomfortable and 'jokes' that are offensive even if some guys think they're harmless. It may not happen to you, but it's worth knowing how to deal with it if it does.

definitions

{ SEXUAL HARASSMENT }
bullying of a sexual nature that can include verbal or physical unwelcome sexual advances, gestures and acts.

The question is why do some boys do this? Well, for some it's a power trip. They do it so they can feel in control and get a response from girls. For others they think it's funny and don't even realise it's unacceptable behaviour (especially if their friends laugh and egg them on). Other boys do it because it's part of the lad culture they have been bought up in and they can't see that their behaviour is offensive and threatening.

If this kind of harassment ever happens to you, you don't necessarily have to speak out there and then. In fact, in

the big issue!

HARASSMENT IN A RELATIONSHIP

Everyone has a right to feel respected and safe in a relationship and if at some point in your life you don't, you should speak up about it and find help. While physical abuse is an obvious sign, there are many other signs of being in a problematic relationship, such as:

* Being told that if you don't do something your boyfriend will dump you/spread rumours about you/send something to your parents.

* Being called names, such as fat/silly/ugly.

* Being controlled. If your boyfriend reads your messages, has access to your social media pages, or tells you who you can and can't follow or see as friends.

* Being told what to do, what to wear, who to see, how to behave when you're out.

some cases it's really important that you don't, particularly if you are on your own or there is the slightest chance that the situation could get worse. Plus when you experience harassment, it's common to feel fear, embarrassment, shame, or shock and panic. This means it's often difficult to respond and take action at the time it happens.

In this case, finding your voice means telling someone what has happened to you so action can be taken to stop it if it keeps happening. It's about seeking help (see 'Be the change on page 126-127) if you don't know how to make it stop. It's also worth bearing in mind that there is no time limit to finding your voice. If something bothers you but it happened a while ago, you can still talk about what happened whenever you need to.

your voice and the issue of consent

What is consent and what has it got to do with being a girl? Well, quite a lot really. In reality every act you do with someone requires consent, even if it's holding hands or kissing. Consent in this

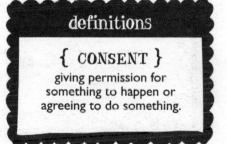

definitions

{ CONSENT }
giving permission for something to happen or agreeing to do something.

case means that both people in a situation agree to do it and either person may decide at any time that they no longer consent and want to stop doing it.

What's more, consenting to one activity does not mean you consent to more, even if you're dating and even if you thought you wanted to do it. And consenting on one

continues on page 124

be the boss of you!

FINDING YOUR VOICE

Finding your voice isn't easy. Maybe you're shy or hate speaking in front of others. Perhaps you think no one will listen or you have nothing to say. These are all common fears that we all go through whether we're young or old, female or male. That is why it's worth bearing in mind there are many ways to have a voice.

1 You can have a voice online via social media such as Twitter or blogging. You can have a voice by joining a campaigning organisation (see 'Be the change on page 126-127), by speaking up in class or speaking out at school about something you believe in. And of course, you can have a voice just by getting involved and voting in elections at school.

2 Get impassioned about things that you think are unjust or that make you angry in life. Is there something that makes you feel judged?

Or is there something in life that makes you wish you were older so you could do something? It's the things that you feel passionate about that can help you to find your voice and make a stand for something you believe in. There are all sorts of ways to be involved. If you get angry about double standards, for example, you could join the Everyday Sexism campaign (see page 113 and 'Be the change' pages 126-127), or if you feel strongly about endangered animals you could become part of the WWF campaign to help save them.

occasion also does not mean you have to consent again or that consent is not needed again.

what is the age of consent?

In the United Kingdom, the age of consent is 16. This is the legal age when the law says that you are mature enough to be able to agree to have sex if you want to. In most countries, until you reach this age you can't legally have sex with anyone, however old they are, even if you want to.

Consent is about finding and using your voice and being able to say no to any activity that you don't want to do. This includes being sent or being asked to send 'selfies' that you feel uncomfortable about or sexts. Remember, even if your friends say they do it, it's your right to say NO as loudly as you can!

being a girl with a strong voice

By now I hope you realise that liking yourself and standing up for yourself is the key to feeling strong and amazing as a girl. If you can walk around knowing you're wonderful, bold, brave and daring that's how others will see you and that's how they will treat you too. Not only will this empower you, but it will also make you feel strong and capable, no matter where you are, or what you do.

So make sure that:

❊ You feel good about yourself for at least 85% of the time!

❊ You work at being happy with your body no matter what size or shape you are.

❊ You find a voice to talk about the things in life that make you feel upset, frustrated and impassioned!

❊ You believe you can make a difference even in small ways.

❊ You do the things YOU want to do in life, not what you think you should be doing.

❊ You have the courage to try things you're afraid of on a regular basis.

❊ You are the boss of you in major life decisions!

❊ You question what you believe especially if it's making you unhappy.

❊ You surround yourself with people who have similar values to you.

❊ You remind yourself that being a girl is the best thing in the world.

be the change!

Books, websites and useful organisations:

abuse

thisisabuse.direct.gov.uk
Help, information and support about relationship abuse including emotional, physical and verbal abuse.

anxiety

Anxiety UK
anxietyuk.org.uk
Anxiety UK works to relieve and support those living with anxiety disorders by providing information, support and understanding via an extensive range of services, including 1:1 therapy.

beat

b-eat.co.uk
Eating disorders help and information, and support for anyone suffering from an eating disorder or worried about one.

bethany hamilton

http://bethanyhamilton. com
Pro-surfing champion, who lost an arm in a shark attack and now works to help and inspire others.

body image

MediaSmart
mediasmart.org.uk
Free of charge educational materials to primary schools, which teach children to think critically about advertising in the context of their daily lives.

bullying

bullying.co.uk
Help, advice and information on bullying and cyberbullying.

childline

0800 1111
childline.org.uk
For help and advice on a wide range of issues. You can talk to a confidential counsellor online by sending ChildLine an email or by posting on the message boards.

cyberbullying

stopcyberbullying.org
This organisation works to relieve and support those living with anxiety disorders by providing information, support and understanding via an extensive range of services, including 1:1 therapy.

end violence against women

endviolnceagainst women.org.uk
End Violence Against Women is a coalition of organisations and individuals campaigning to end all forms of violence against women.

empowerment

Who Needs Feminism
whoneedsfeminism. tumblr.com
A brilliant view of why teen girls need feminism.

everyday sexism

www.everydaysexism. com
The Everyday Sexism Project exists to catalogue instances of sexism experienced by women and girls on a day-to-day basis. They might be serious or minor, outrageously offensive or so niggling and normalised that you don't even feel able to protest. By sharing your story you're showing the world that sexism does exist, it is faced by women everyday and it is a valid problem to discuss.

equality

www.fawcettsociety.org. uk
The UK's leading campaign for women's equality at home, at work and in public life.

family lives

0808 800 2222
familylives.org.uk
A help and advice organisation for parents and teens on all issues relating to family life.

depression

www.youngminds.org.uk
Offering information and support if you're feeling depressed and suicidal.

kidscape

www.kidscape.org.uk
Advice and help on everything from bullying to making friends and worries and anxieties.

love is louder

http://www.loveis louder.com
To support anyone feeling mistreated, misunderstood or alone. It's hundreds of thousands of people just like you who have turned this idea into a movement.

malala fund

www.malalafund.org
Around the world, girls are denied a formal education because of social, economic, legal and political factors. And in being denied an education, society loses one of its greatest and most powerful resources. The Malala Fund aims to change that.

a mighty girl

www.amightygirl.com
A brilliant site about books, films and more that is dedicated to smart, confident girls.

national eating disorders association

nationaleating disorders.org
Helping with all eating disorders across all ages.

one billion rising

onebillionrising.org
This is a global call to women survivors of violence and those who love them to gather safely outside places where they are entitled to justice – courthouses, police stations, government offices, school administration buildings, work places, sites of environmental injustice, military courts, embassies, places of worship, homes, or simply public gathering places - where women deserve to feel safe but too often do not.

puberty

beinggirl.co.uk
Information and facts about periods and puberty.

rape crisis

0808 802 9999
rapecrisis.org.uk
Rape Crisis (England and Wales) campaigns to raise awareness of sexual violence and the need for high-quality and specialised support for survivors.

self-esteem

Campaign for Real Beauty Dove dove.co.uk
The self-esteem project from Dove, which focuses on body image, self-esteem and mothers and daughters.

self-harm

youngminds.org.uk
For help, advice and support.

sexting

NSPCC nspcc.org.uk
Search for sexting when you reach the home page.

teen feminist

http://www.teenfeminist. com
Feminism from a teen perspective.

smart girls

https://www.facebook.com
A great Facebook page worth following (you need to look it up or search on Facebook) all about encouragement and confidence.

think u know

thinkuknow.co.uk
How to stay safe online.

vagenda

vagendamag.blogspot.co.uk
A blog discussing feminism, women's rights and sexism in the media.

index